Everything You Need to Know About

Cliques

Friendships are increasingly important during one's high school years, but cliques can sometimes cause divisions.

Everything You Need to Know About

Cliques

Heather Moehn

The Rosen Publishing Group, Inc.
New York

Published in 2001 by The Rosen Publishing Group, Inc.
29 East 21st Street, New York, NY 10010

Copyright © 2001 by The Rosen Publishing Group, Inc.

First Edition

Library of Congress Cataloging-in-Publication Data

Moehn, Heather.
    Everything you need to know about cliques / by Heather Moehn—1st ed.
       p. cm.—(Need to know library)
    Includes bibliographical references and index.
    ISBN 0-8239-3326-1
    1. Interpersonal relations in adolescence—Juvenile literature. 2. Cliques (Sociology)—Juvenile literature. 3. Friendship in adolescence—Juvenile literature. [1. Cliques (Sociology). 2. Social groups. 3. Interpersonal relations. 4. Friendship.] I. Title. II. Series.
BF724.3.I58 M64 2000
158.2'5—dc21

                        00-010320

Contents

Cliques can cause divisions at school—particularly in the cafeteria.

Introduction

As Diana carried her tray through the crowded cafeteria, she looked at all the different tables. The same groups of people sat in the same places every day. The jocks and cheerleaders sat together in the center of the room. The computer geeks were at another table, while the burnouts and goths sat at separate tables in the back. The African-American kids always sat at the table nearest the exit.

Lorraine, Diana's lab partner in biology, was a goth. Diana thought Lorraine was really nice and knew she would enjoy hanging out with her, but she felt too strange to walk up to their table. She knew that if she did, everyone would stare at her and wonder what she was doing. Diana didn't

*want to deal with the pressure, so she walked over
to her own group of friends, put down her tray,
and began to eat.*

Divisions, such as those in Diana's lunchroom, exist every day in high schools across the country. Students often separate into groups based upon their interests, what they wear, where they hang out, and common activities in which they participate. Other times they are identified by the color of their skin or their families' economic class. These groups are commonly known as cliques.

The basic definition of a clique is a small, exclusive group of people. But to most teenagers, cliques mean much more than that. As teens become more independent, friends often act as a family away from home. They provide support and acceptance and let you know that what you are thinking and feeling is okay. Becoming part of a clique is also a way of establishing your identity and defining who you are.

Despite these good points, cliques often make life very difficult for many teens. For everyone who feels like a secure part of a group, there is someone who feels left out and ignored. Relationships in cliques can be fickle. You may feel as if you don't know who your true friends are. You might hide parts of your personality in order to be accepted, or give up a certain goal or ambition that the group doesn't see as cool.

Introduction

Whether you love cliques or hate them, they are probably going to be around as long as junior high and high school exist. Indeed, many experts feel that inclusion in a social group is an important part of growing up and helps prepare teens for life as adults. This book will show you how to handle various issues about friends, both at school and at home. Although you can't get rid of cliques, you can learn how to make navigating your social life a little easier.

In the first few chapters we will explore what cliques are, why they form, and why people feel the need to belong. We will also look at the role of friendship in your life and how your friendships change as you get older. Then we will examine how cliques are viewed by other students, teachers, and school administrators. We will also take a close look at the myths and facts surrounding popularity, and explain why popularity and friendship are not the same thing.

Sometimes your friends begin to do things you don't agree with, such as drinking, doing drugs, or shoplifting. Or you may feel that they don't allow you to be yourself and that you have to act a certain way around them. When this happens, it may be time to leave the group and find new friends. We will explore ways to handle this delicate issue and provide tips on making new friends.

Many major disagreements between teens and their families revolve around friends. This book will help you learn to balance your social life with the demands of your family. We will also provide some insight into why your parents all of sudden don't like you spending time with your friends and what they fear when you are a part of a clique.

Finally, we will explore what often happens to friendships after high school and how the friends you have now will help form the basis for making lasting friendships in the future.

Chapter One | How Friendships Develop

When you were a toddler, you probably played with whoever was around. Your playmates may have been the children of your parents' friends, or kids who lived in your neighborhood. It didn't matter to you whether the friends were boys or girls or what race or religion they were. At that age, you were learning how to interact with people your own age and how to share.

Around the time you entered kindergarten, you may remember gravitating toward friends of your own gender. While you began to make more meaningful friendships, family was still the center of your life. If something was bothering you or you had good news, you usually couldn't wait to tell your parents. They helped you through all the good and bad times of your life.

Young kids usually interact easily with others.

As you entered adolescence, the dependency you previously had upon your family probably changed. Your friends probably began to play a much more important role, taking the place of your family as the center of your life. You may have turned to friends instead of family members when faced with problems. Most likely, you also began to base your identity on your friends instead of family. Perhaps you got a tattoo or a body piercing, dyed your hair, or starting dressing like all your friends against your parents' wishes. Or you may have pulled away from family in more fundamental ways, such as rejecting the religion you grew up with or turning away from your ethnic heritage.

Romantic Relationships

During junior high and high school, romantic relationships begin to develop. This throws a whole new twist on friendships. For both boys and girls, dating can have a positive effect on friendships with members of their own sex. It can be something to talk about, strategize about, celebrate, or despair over. But dating can also have a negative effect. Friends might become jealous about the amount of time you spend with your significant other and might be afraid that their relationship with you will change because of the new person in your life.

At first, Debbie thought it was fun when her friend Tanya started dating Paul. They stayed up late, trying new hairstyles and make-up tricks to make Tanya look more sophisticated. They gossiped about what Paul said to Tanya between classes and pored over the notes he left in her locker.

But then Tanya started seeing much more of Paul and began to cancel plans she had made with Debbie. She would only do something with Debbie if Paul had other plans on his own. Debbie felt hurt that Tanya was willing to throw away all the years they were best friends for a guy, and soon stopped calling her.

You may feel left out if your friends begin to date before you do.

Dating someone might make you part of a new clique. You might suddenly feel more popular and have many more friends. However, it's important that the new group accepts you on your own terms, instead of simply as so-and-so's girlfriend or boyfriend. Otherwise, if you break up with the person, you could also be breaking up with the clique.

What if you like someone who is outside your clique and your friends don't approve? There are many books and movies with plots about this very topic because it happens quite often and can pose some tough questions. The approval of friends is important to everyone, but friends don't always know what is best for you. If you are in this situation, try to

14

Dating someone outside of your clique can be complicated.

bring your significant other to a few group events. Hopefully when your friends get to know him or her, they will see why you want to date the person and stop giving you a hard time about it.

However, if they still don't accept him or her, you may be in the tough position of having to choose. You might decide that your friends are too important to lose over a guy or girl, or you might decide that if your friends can't accept the person you are dating, then they aren't really true friends.

Chapter Two | The Formation of Cliques

Kids begin rejecting other kids as early as preschool, and by kindergarten, they have a sense of who is popular and who is not. The earliest signs of cliques usually appear in second grade. Cliques become more noticeable in fourth grade, and then dominate students' lives in junior high.

Gender and Friendships

Most psychologists believe that boys and girls view friendships differently. Girls typically split into cliques at age eleven, when the more mature girls begin puberty. When describing their friends, girls talk about character traits such as loyalty, sharing, and being thoughtful and considerate. Girls are more likely to

Many kids, especially boys, base their early friendships on shared activities, such as sports.

have one or two best friends at a time. They are also more likely to participate in and be hurt by cruel remarks and gossip.

Boys' cliques tend to form a little later, typically around age thirteen or fourteen, when interests are more defined. Boys tend to focus on activities and doing things together, such as fishing or playing sports. Instead of one or two best friends, boys often have a small group of friends that isn't as fixed—if one friend can't play basketball one day, another can substitute. When describing friends, most boys speak about skill at sports, bravery, and a sense of humor or adventure. Boys are not as aware of appearances and don't usually bother with rumors or who-likes-whom gossip.

Pros and Cons of Cliques

Cliques are most common in large urban or suburban high schools where the number of students makes it easier to form subgroups. In a large school, cliques can provide a sense of stability in a constantly changing environment. They can also make the school seem more friendly and personal by providing a close knit group of friends who stick by your side.

There are many other positive aspects of being in a clique, such as having close friends with the same interests and background as you. Friends in a clique will probably understand things about you that no one else does. It helps to talk to friends about the things that happen in your life. By talking to them, you learn that your fears, concerns, and feelings are normal. You also might use your friends as models and mirrors to find out what is socially acceptable and what makes people well liked. Since adolescence is a time of discovering your identity, a clique can help you figure out who you are. And friends in a clique may challenge you to try new things and see issues from a different point of view.

Katherine's friends were the most important thing in the world to her. She felt as if they totally understood her. All of them had grown up in the same neighborhood and came from similar backgrounds.

A clique can be positive when it provides you with a group of friends you can confide in.

When Katherine's parents decided to get divorced, she didn't know what to do. She had so many fears and a lot of anger and guilt. The parents of one of her close friends, Sue, had gotten divorced two years before. Sue was able to help Katherine understand what was happening and to realize that it wasn't her fault. Katherine felt like she would be lost without Sue.

There are also many bad things about cliques. You might feel that the people in your clique really don't understand you and that you are growing apart from them. At some point, you may realize that the friends you hang out with aren't people you want to be like.

You might feel as if the clique is holding you back from trying new things and learning new things about yourself. It is common to realize that you want different things in life than what your friends want.

Jamil had serious doubts about his group of friends junior year. All of them had gone to the same junior high, then became really close when they entered high school. Since four junior high schools feed into the high school, his class size more than quadrupled. It was easy to get lost those first weeks, so Jamil and his friends stuck together.

Now, however, he was beginning to question their friendship. Jamil knew he wanted to go to college—a good four-year school. But his friends really weren't concerned with grades or extracurricular activities. They couldn't understand why Jamil would want to do volunteer work after school some days, or why he spent so much time studying. When Jamil was with them, he felt pressure to slack off and not try his hardest.

It wasn't like that with Mark, a guy he met while volunteering at an animal shelter. Mark also wanted to go to college and was concerned about grades and doing well in school. Jamil really liked Mark and wanted to spend more time with him, but he knew his friends would give him a hard time. They would say stuff like, "Why do you want to hang out with that brainy dweeb? We're much more fun."

Jamil really felt torn. He knew he would enjoy getting to know Mark better, but didn't know how to without causing major problems with his clique of friends.

Chapter Three | Cliques and Popularity

In many schools, certain cliques are considered more "popular" than others. Often the school administration will treat certain groups, such as the athletes, better than less popular students because these groups make the school look good to the public. When this happens, the students who are not part of these cliques often complain about the preferential treatment popular students receive. This results in tension between groups.

Last month there was a huge party at some kid's house while his parents were away. It was a really cool party. People from all different groups were there. But it got so huge and out of control that it was busted by the cops and everyone was charged with underage possession of alcohol.

Our school has a strict no-drug policy, so we knew we would all be punished in some way. I play the saxophone in the band and had to miss the all-state competition because of the party. This is a once-a-year opportunity—I have only four chances in high school to make it. I had worked all year for it.

Four of the starters on the boys' basketball team were at the party too. The team has a good chance of winning the championship this year, but without those four, they wouldn't do as well in the regular season. The guys had to sit out one game. One game! I had to miss tryouts for the musical equivalent of the state basketball tournament, and all they had to do was miss one game. It definitely wasn't fair, but basketball rules the school and there is no way that the school would jeopardize its chances of being in the state tournament.

The fact that preferential treatment is given to certain groups is becoming more evident as students involved in school shootings often target the more popular groups. Fortunately, in the wake of events such as the shootings at Columbine High School in Littleton, Colorado, school officials are beginning to realize the harm that can result when people are treated differently. Some schools now hold pep rallies not just for athletics, but also for music contests, theater productions, and debate competitions.

In general, many experts believe that high school students are more tolerant of differences than they were a generation ago. Another positive change in recent years is that more students than ever before think of themselves as popular. The Sloan Study of Youth and Social Development by Barbara Schneider and David Stevenson found that 10 percent of students considered themselves very popular, 65 percent thought they were somewhat popular, and 25 percent felt they were not popular. They found that there are fewer "elite" crowds that everyone wants to be a part of. Instead, there are smaller social groups whose membership often changes over the course of high school.

What Is Popularity?

Everyone wants to be liked and respected and to have lots of close friends. Being accepted into a popular clique may seem very important to you. You may think that all your social problems will be solved if you only had the right group of friends. However, popularity is not as great as many people think. Often people who seem popular have just as many doubts and fears as those who do not consider themselves popular.

Think about popularity in terms of singers. Who was your favorite singer three years ago? Is he or she still around? Is he or she still popular? Most likely not. Popularity is a very fickle thing. Just because someone

Popularity and friendship are not necessarily the same thing.

is popular one year doesn't mean that he or she will be viewed that way next year. The same goes for unpopular people. There is no reason someone can't become more popular as time goes by.

Also keep in mind that popularity is not the same thing as friendship. Friendship is being close to someone with whom you have a history, someone you can talk to about meaningful events in your life. Popularity is when a group decides you have some traits that they like and consider important.

Myths About Popularity

There are many myths about popularity and what makes someone popular. Maybe you believe some of them. If so, it may be worth re-evaluating what being popular means to you and why you want to be part of the "in crowd."

Myth #1: Popularity Equals Happiness

Although popular people may always seem to be having a terrific time and have lots of friends to do fun things with, what appears on the surface isn't always true. As we discussed earlier, popularity isn't a sure thing. Popular people might feel incredible pressure to remain popular. Often that can mean acting in ways that they don't feel comfortable with, or doing things they don't really want to. There is always a fear that they will lose their popularity and people will see that they aren't as great as they seem.

Marissa was one of the most popular people in the senior class. Everyone knew who she was and she always created a stir when she walked in a room. When her parents divorced, Marissa's mother got to keep their huge house on the outskirts of town. In order to keep up the house and continue to buy Marissa all the best clothes and whatever else she wanted, Marissa's mother had to take on a better-paying job. As a result, she was out of town a lot on business.

One weekend while her mother was away, Marissa invited a few friends over. Soon word got out that there was a party, and close to a hundred people showed up with lots of alcohol. Since there were no neighbors close by and no adults to supervise, everyone thought it was a great party. Now whenever her mother leaves town, Marissa throws another huge bash. She feels like all her friends expect her to and that they won't like her if she doesn't. She doesn't like watching people trash her house, but is afraid that if she tells them "no," they will no longer want to hang out with her.

Myth #2: Popularity Gives People Self-Confidence

Self-confidence and self-esteem come from inside you. Popularity isn't going to give you confidence if you don't already have it. Although popular people are thought to have great self-confidence, they usually have just as many insecurities and problems as other people. They often work hard to present a more confident image that they feel pressured to maintain. As a result, they are less likely to discuss their fears with friends and more likely to keep bad feelings bottled up. Many times this does more damage to self-esteem than not being popular at all.

Tyler hates all the "Tyler for President" posters hanging in the hallways at school. He is tired of school politics and doesn't really enjoy being involved anymore. However, everyone expected him

Sometimes the pressures of popularity can cause stress.

to run and he felt he didn't really have a choice. Everyone thinks he would make the perfect president, but Tyler isn't so sure. How could they not see that he doesn't really know what he is doing? He is terrified of making bad decisions. What if he blows the student budget? What if other projects don't work out? Tyler is really worried that he won't be able to handle the responsibility.

Myth #3: Popular People Have More Friends and Better Friendships

Some people—say a star football player or a beautiful girl who seems really sophisticated—gain popularity because of what they do or who they seem to be. As a result, they may be surrounded by people who want a little of that image to rub off on them. They don't bother to get to know who the popular person is on the inside. Although a popular person may party a lot and always has people surrounding him or her, it isn't the number of friends that counts, it is the depth of the friendships. And often depth is lacking.

Mariah moved to Minneapolis from New York City when her father was transferred. Her mother was from Argentina and Mariah's dark hair and olive complexion seemed very exotic to the mostly fair-skinned midwesterners. She had the latest trendy clothes from New York and her street savvy made her seem very hip. She instantly fell in with the popular crowd, and all the girls started imitating the way she dressed and wore her hair.

Even though she was always surrounded by people as she walked through the halls, Mariah felt very lonely. She felt as if people only liked her for the image she presented. She missed her friends from New York who knew about her history and who she was on the inside. Nobody here seemed to care what she was like on the inside. They only wanted to be more like Mariah was on the outside.

Myth #4: Everybody Likes Popular People

Being truly well liked is something that has to be earned. It comes from caring about other people, taking

Taking a sincere interest in others will allow you to develop deep, meaningful friendships.

a genuine interest in others, and being confident in your own abilities. It may appear as if everyone likes the popular people in your school, but take a close look at why they seem well liked. Do people really like who the popular person is, or do they like the external factors that make that person popular (such as a great talent at football)? Being truly well liked does not come instantly with popularity. It is something that takes work.

Derek worked in the movie theater box office. His friends always expected him to let them in for free and get them into R-rated movies. For a while, he didn't mind sneaking them in. He enjoyed all the attention his friends gave him.

But after a while he began to get nervous. The manager started watching him more, especially when kids his age were in line. Plus he was upset that his friends always expected him to let them in no matter what. One weekend he told his friends that they had to pay from now on and that he couldn't give them tickets for R-rated movies. When they complained, he said the manager had told him he would lose his job if he kept doing it. Unfortunately, many of his friends got mad and stopped talking to him. But a few people stuck by him and became even better friends after the group split up.

Chapter Four | Misfits, Bullying, and Harassment

An unfortunate result of some cliques being popular is that other cliques will be labeled unpopular. This distinction is usually made with a shallow definition of the word "popular." If you feel you don't fit in at your high school, it does not mean that you will feel like that for the rest of your life. In fact, many people who have made an impact on the world were not popular in high school.

Lora Brody, a famous cookbook writer, describes her high school experience in her book *Growing Up on the Chocolate Diet*:

> *In my high school, popularity was unfortunately not based on one's ability to bake a wicked brownie. . . . Cheerleaders with big breasts, nice*

teeth, and naturally curly hair got dates. . . . Being short and skinny with braces and glasses, I was basically ignored by all my heartthrobs.

Harassment

Sometimes the popular groups don't just ignore the less popular students. Sometimes they bully and harass them. The powerful groups often feel that they have a right to pick on and bother people who don't belong to their group. This can create a hostile environment and make school a difficult place for many people. Adding to the problem is that when the bullies are the school's elite students, teachers and administrators often turn a blind eye to such issues.

> *My friends and I totally rule the school. We are really great football players and basically we can get away with anything. I don't know why, but we always pick on this one kid. He's really overweight and the main thing to do in homeroom is tease him. When he gets upset he scrunches up his fat face and it's really funny. The homeroom teacher is our coach so he just ignores what is going on.*

Bullies are usually motivated by a sense of power and control that they feel when picking on people. They like to know that they can get whatever they want, whenever they want it. In many cases, this is motivated by the worries and insecurities most adolescents deal with. The bullies might think, "If I pick on this dork, then people won't notice that I'm an even bigger dork."

Many of the recent school shootings were carried out by students who were bullied by other students. Violence is never a good answer and only serves to create more pain and anger in people. If you are thinking about being violent to yourself or others, or feel depressed, talk to

Tips on How to Deal with Bullies

Don't be an easy target—Your body language tells a bully whether you are vulnerable or not. When you stand up straight, talk in a loud, clear voice, and make eye contact with the bully, you show him or her that you are not vulnerable.

Avoid isolated places—Bullies are more likely to cause trouble if you are alone in a place where no one can see or hear you.

Watch for trouble—At the first sign of bullying, try to deflect it with humor or by changing the subject.

Find a close group of friends—The saying that there is safety in numbers is true. If you and your friends stick together and protect each other, bullies are less likely to view you as a target.

Although they act tough, bullies are often motivated by feelings of insecurity.

someone. Parents, friends, siblings, school counselors, and teachers are there to help. If you don't feel comfortable talking with them, there are a number of hotlines in the back of this book that specialize in helping people who are feeling depressed.

What If You Are Being Harassed?

If you are the victim of bullying and harassment, try not to show that it bothers you. If the bullies think you don't care what they do, they may move on to another target. You could also bring the problem to the attention of the school administrators. Maybe they could move your locker or switch your schedule so you don't have to see the bullies as often during the day. Just remember that high school does not last forever (although it may feel like

Think about the consequences of your actions before you try to bully someone.

it at times). Soon you will be in college or working and will have plenty of opportunities to meet people with the same interests as you. After high school, people are generally more accepting of others—or at least are willing to choose their friends based on less shallow criteria.

What If You Are the Bully?

If you are one of the bullies, stop and think about what the possible results of your actions might be. Remember that being cruel does not make you a more powerful or better person. Try to put yourself in the other person's place. Would you like to constantly confront harassment? (You should also keep in mind that one of the computer "geeks" or math "nerds" you are picking on today may turn out to be your boss someday in the future!)

Chapter Five | When It May Be Time to Leave a Clique

Peer pressure is a daily part of life for teenagers. Sometimes the pressure can be good, such as when friends push each other to excel in sports or academics. But many times it can be a really negative factor in your life. If your friends constantly pressure you to do things that you clearly feel uncomfortable about, such as drinking, doing drugs, and having sex, they are not true friends.

What Is Peer Pressure?

Peer pressure can take many forms. It can be as open as someone saying, "Don't be such a goody-goody" or "Everybody's doing it." Or, it can be more subtle, such as unvoiced expectations by your friends about how to

Real friends don't try to pressure you to do things after you have clearly said no.

dress, act, or treat other people. Either way, if it is something you don't want to do or that goes against your personal or societal values, it is important to make the decision that is right for you.

Standing Up for Yourself

Your friends may be pressuring you because they are unsure about themselves. Often, people who doubt themselves in a situation will put pressure on others to do the same thing. They believe that if everyone else is doing it too, then it is okay. During high-pressure moments, it is very difficult to keep your own principles in sight. One way to feel more confident at these times is to think beforehand about what you will say.

Kirsten, a fifteen-year-old sophomore, had decided that she never wanted to smoke. A few of her friends began smoking and offered her cigarettes whenever they were together. At first she was very uncomfortable and didn't know what to say, but then she thought about it. The next time she was offered cigarettes she simply said, "No, thanks. My grandfather died of lung cancer. I really don't want to smoke." Her friends respected that, and soon they even stopped smoking around her.

Unfortunately, you might not be as lucky as Kirsten. Your friends might begin to put more pressure on you or get angry with you. They might feel like you are judging them and resent you for that. Again, it might seem easier to simply go along with the crowd. It takes a lot of courage to stand up for yourself if what you think is different from what your friends think.

It is important to consider your self-esteem. You probably are happy being a part of a clique and like to feel popular and well liked. However, do you really feel good about yourself if you are participating in activities you know are wrong, or ignoring parts of yourself because you are worried that your friends won't think you are cool? Self-esteem comes from being true to yourself and your beliefs.

The best way to be well liked is to simply be yourself.

Many people, when they talk about being popular, advise that you should "Just be yourself." To many teens, this sounds like nonsense. How can you just be yourself when you aren't sure who that person is? What it means is that if you figure out how you want to act and stick with it, you are going to gain more confidence in yourself than someone who blindly goes along with the crowd. And self-confidence is one of the biggest factors in determining if someone is well liked or not.

Chapter Six | Making New Friends

Leaving a group of friends, even if it is the right thing to do, is very difficult. There is comfort and security in staying with people you already know and who already know you. Depending on your reasons for leaving, you may be able to still do things with your old group of friends while trying to make other new friends. If you feel you need a complete break, there may be a period of loneliness as you feel out other people and as they get to know you. Remember that good friendships are based on trust, and that is something that can only be gained over time.

Hint #1: Relax!

One reason people find it difficult to make friends is because they fear rejection. Many are so afraid of being

Making new friends can be less difficult if you remember to relax and remain approachable.

turned away that they don't even try to become friends with people they admire and would like to get to know better. So, the first step in making new friends is to relax and realize that everyone else feels the same way. Even people who seem as if they have great friends may worry that someone new won't like them.

Hint #2: Be Approachable

If you are always surrounded by the same group of friends, it will seem as if you aren't trying to meet new people, and others will stay away. Likewise, if you give off signals that you don't want to be disturbed, such as never making eye contact or keeping your head down when walking through the halls, people won't try to talk to you. To look like you are interested in meeting someone, catch his or her eye and smile.

You should also try to talk with him or her. This doesn't mean you have to blurt out a major statement like, "Hi, I think you are nice and would like to be your friend." It can be as simple as walking out of math class with someone and asking, "Did you understand that last problem?" It isn't easy, but if you take the first steps, you may find a wonderful new group of friends.

Last year, Grace's locker was two down from Elizabeth's. Elizabeth was a starting player on the girls' basketball team. Grace had always admired

Elizabeth's easygoing attitude and hilarious sense of humor and thought she would be a great person to become friends with.

One morning, when they were both collecting their books for the first period class, Grace got up the courage to talk to Elizabeth. "What time is the game tonight?" she asked. Elizabeth answered, "Do you mean ours or the boys'? They are playing across town, which means no one will be at our game." That night Grace convinced her group of friends to go to the girls' game instead of the boys'.

The next morning Elizabeth rushed over to Grace's locker. "Thanks for coming last night! It was so great to have people cheering for us." They began talking more and more between classes and ended up hanging out together after school once in a while. Now, a year later, they are great friends and hope to room together next year at the state university.

Hint #3: Get Involved

Another way to meet new people is to join a new activity or group that seems interesting. It could be something organized at school, such as a theater group, debate club, or the yearbook committee. Or it could be something outside of school such as a part-time job, a church-sponsored youth group, or a volunteer activity.

Tips on Making New Friends

◆ Say "Hi" to people you don't know very well when you pass them in the hall.

◆ When someone talks to you, focus on him or her. Don't look over his or her shoulder to see who else is going by.

◆ Join a club or team that interests you.

◆ Make sure your body language is open and friendly—smile, make eye contact, and keep your shoulders relaxed.

◆ Look past appearances. You wouldn't want someone judging you based only on how you look, so don't do it to others.

◆ Don't gossip about others. People will find it difficult to trust you if they know you don't always keep secrets and talk about people behind their backs.

There are many benefits to meeting people in this kind of setting. One is that you know you already have one thing in common—the interest in the activity. Another is that it automatically gives you something to talk about. Third, it is easy to have such activities lead to other things. For instance, if you are in the drama club, you will probably have rehearsals after school. It would be much easier to ask people to go out to eat after rehearsal than if you only saw them during the school day.

Steve had played the electric guitar his entire life and really loved it. Since his friends weren't into music at all, he could only play when they didn't have plans. One night at a football game, he noticed a guy in the pep band quietly playing one of his favorite songs on the sidelines. Steve approached him and asked if he was in a band. "Naw," the sax player said, "I just play around once in a while."

Steve told him that he played the electric guitar and was looking for people to play with. That weekend, the saxophone player and two other people from the band, a drummer and a keyboard player, met in Steve's basement and played for five hours straight. They had so much fun they decided to get together every week. Now Steve has a set of friends who share his interest in music.

Chapter Seven | Your Friends and Your Family

Friends are often at the center of many arguments between teenagers and their families. One of the common reasons for this tension is the parents' belief that their teen is spending too much time with his or her friends. Another common source of trouble is a parent's disapproval of a child's friends or significant other.

Despite the perception that teens spend huge amounts of time with their friends, the Sloan study found that most teens today spend more time alone. The researchers found that out of their waking hours, teens spend 43 percent of time in school, 20 percent alone, 19 percent with their families, 4 percent working, and only 9 percent with their friends outside of school.

All this free time spent alone can make teens feel very lonely. A clique can fill this loneliness and provide emotional support that might be missing in families in which both parents work outside the home, in smaller families with fewer children, and in single-parent households, which are becoming more common as the rate of divorce increases.

My friend Tuan and I like to study geometry together. When we talk about the problems together we both seem to understand them better. I would probably be flunking if it weren't for our study sessions. Tuan plays on the tennis team, which practices after school. Because of that, we have to get together to study after dinner. We usually study about three times a week.

My mom has been getting really upset lately because I am spending so much time with Tuan. She says that I am never home anymore. Well, that's just not true. I go home right after school and stay there until after dinner. But she doesn't get home from work until 5:30, so she doesn't even know if I am there or not. Last night we had a huge blowout and I told her that if she wants to see me so badly, she should be home after school. I felt bad, but why does the way I spend my time have to center around her schedule?

Having fights with your parents about friends and how you spend your time is a normal part of the teenage years. Adolescence is a time of separating from your family and becoming an adult. While you are probably ready

Introducing new friends to a parent or stepparent will help to alleviate his or her concerns.

for these changes, your parents may not be. They may not understand why you don't find family outings as fun as you used to or why you would rather spend your free time with friends. They still see you as their child and may be reluctant to give you the freedom you want.

Your parents may be more willing to allow you to spend time with your friends if you do not entirely abandon your family. You may have to make some compromises. For instance, if you eat dinner with you family most nights of the week, they probably won't mind if you go out for pizza with your friends on a Friday night.

Your parents are probably worried that your friends will have a bad influence on you. This will be especially true if they have seen your friends smoking or drinking.

One way you can get them to approve of your friends is to invite your friends over to your house so your parents can meet them. Have your friends over for dinner one night so your parents can talk to them and get to know them a little.

It is also important not to shut your parents completely out of your social life. This doesn't mean you have to tell them everything. But you should tell them where you are going to be—and stick to what you say! Earning your parents' trust is key. Once you have their trust, you should be given more freedom. But remember that trust is much easier to lose than it is to earn. Don't abuse any privileges once you receive them.

Cliques and Siblings

If you have brothers or sisters who are close to you in age, you probably experience sibling rivalry. Sibling rivalry refers to the competition and jealousies that come between brothers and sisters in a family. If you go to the same school as your siblings, there can be rivalry about cliques. It is difficult to be in the shadow of a sibling who is more popular than you. Likewise, having a sibling who is not as popular as you can be embarrassing.

It often helps if your interests and activities are completely separate from those of your sibling. This way, you can be known on your own terms instead of identified with your brother or sister.

Chapter Eight | Cliques After High School

Most people long for a close group of best friends with whom they share everything, like on the TV show *Friends*. They dream about having friends who know and accept everything about them and who will be there forever through anything. The reality, however, is that friends usually come and go as you change and move on in your lives. Chances are, the friends you have right now are different than the friends you had when you were in kindergarten, third grade, and junior high. Your friends will probably change again as you leave high school and go to college or join the work force.

Cliques won't disappear as soon as you graduate from high school. In college, you might join a fraternity or sorority, a club based on your ethnicity, or groups based on your major or interests. In the workforce,

It would be nice if everyone could have a group of pals as supportive as on *Friends*.

people in the same department might become good friends, or you might eat lunch everyday with the same group of people. There are also many organizations through which people in the same profession meet. Most of these groups are less status-oriented or exclusive than cliques in high schools.

Whether or not you stay close to your friends from high school, they have taught you valuable lessons about yourself and others. Because of your clique, you probably have a stronger sense of your identity, values, and habits. You are more independent from your family than when you were younger, and feel more confident in your ability to handle adult responsibilities. Your

There are great friendships that await you after high school.

friends have also taught you how to get along with others, how to listen, and how to stick by someone through the good and the bad times.

If you have had problems with cliques, you know how important it is to stand up for what you believe, how to deal with rejection, and how others should be treated. People who were unpopular in high school often go on to do amazing things in life. Many attribute their success to skills learned while surviving a difficult time during adolescence.

No matter how you feel about cliques, if you learn from your experiences, you will have the ability to make good friends throughout your entire life.

Glossary

body language   Ways of moving or acting that send unspoken signals to other people.

bullying   Picking on or harassing someone.

clique   Small, exclusive group of people who share similar interests.

depression   Feeling upset, unhappy, and hopeless most of the time.

friendship   A relationship marked by closeness and an ability to share secrets and discuss meaningful events in one's life.

individuality   The unique and special traits that make a person who he or she is.

myth   Something that is commonly believed, but that isn't true.

peer pressure   When friends challenge you to do something that you don't feel comfortable with or know is wrong.

popularity   The state of being well liked by many people.

self-confidence   Having a belief in your abilities and skills.

self-esteem   Feeling good about who you are and what you represent to others.

sibling rivalry   When siblings compete against each other.

Where to Go for Help

Organizations

In the United States

Global Youth ACTION Network
211 E. 43rd Street, Suite 905
New York, NY 10017
(212) 661-6111
e-mail: gyan@youthlink.org
Web site: http://www.youthlink.org

National Network for Youth
1319 F Street NW, Suite 401
Washington, DC 20004
(202) 783-7949
e-mail: NN4Youth@worldnet.att.net
Web site: http://www.nn4youth.org

In Canada

Alberta Native Friendship Centre Association
10025-106 Street, Suite 1102
Edmonton, Alberta T5J 1G4
(780) 423-3138
e-mail: anfca@nativecentres.org
Web site: http://www.nativecentres.org

Teen Tempo
205 McNabb Street, 3rd Floor
Sault Saint Marie, ON P6B 1Y3

Hotlines

Boys and Girls Town USA
(800) 448-3000

National Crisis Prevention Institute
(800) 558-8976

National Drug and Alcohol Information Treatment
and Referral
(800) 662-HELP [4357]

Youth Crisis and Runaway Hotline
(800) 342-7472

Web Sites

Adolescent Adulthood
http://www.adolescentadulthood.com

Teen Advice Online
http://www.teenadviceonline.org

Teen Aide
http://www.teenaide.org

YES! International
http://www.yesintl.com

For Further Reading

Carlson, Richard. *Don't Sweat the Small Stuff for Teens.* New York: Hyperion Books, 2000.

Fenwick, Elizabeth, and Dr. Tony Smith. *Adolescence: The Survival Guide for Parents and Teenagers.* New York: Dorling Kindersley, 1994.

Gaines, Donna. *Teenage Wasteland: Suburbia's Dead End Kids.* Chicago: University of Chicago Press, 1998.

Kaplan, Leslie S. *Coping with Peer Pressure.* New York: The Rosen Publishing Group, 1983.

Kirberger, Kimberly. *On Friendship.* Deerfield Beach, FL: Health Communications, 2000.

Rubin, Lillian B. *Just Friends: The Role of Friendship in Our Lives.* New York: Harper and Row, 1985.

Schneider, Barbara, and David Stevenson. *The Ambitious Generation: America's Teenagers, Motivated but Directionless.* New Haven: Yale University Press, 1999.

Schneider, Meg F. *Popularity Has Its Ups and Downs.* Englewood Cliffs, NJ: Julian Messner, 1991.

Stefoff, Rebecca. *Adolescence.* New York: Chelsea House Publishers, 1990.

Wesson, Carolyn. *Teen Troubles.* New York: Walker and Company, 1988.

Yager, Jan. *Friendshifts: The Power of Friendship and How It Shapes Our Lives.* Stamford, CT: Hannacroix Creek Books, 1999.

Index

Index

About the Author

Heather Moehn is a freelance writer and editor in Boston. Her nonfiction young adult books cover such diverse topics as world holidays and leukemia. This is her fourth book for young adults.

Photo Credits

Cover photo © Telegraph Colour Library/FPG International; p. 2 © Super Stock; pp. 6, 14, 30, 36, 38, 50 by Michelle Edwards; p. 12 © Arthur Tilley/FPG International; pp. 15, 53 © Everett Collection; p. 17 © Jim Cummins/FPG International; pp. 19, 40 © Telegraph Colour Library/FPG International; p. 25 © VCG/FPG International; p. 28 by Brian Silak; p. 30 by David Brody; p. 35 by Daniel Brody; p. 43 © Navaswan/FPG International; p. 54 © Ken Chernus/FPG International.

Layout

Laura Murawski